Leadership Mastery:

Unlock Your Full Potential and Lead with Impact

By Dennis Mullins, MBA

Dennis Mullins
Celina, TX

DEDICATION

To my dearest Audrey,

This book, "Leadership Mastery: Unlock Your Full Potential and Lead With Impact," is dedicated to you, my love, my partner in all things adventurous and extraordinary. You have been my rock, my confidante, and my biggest cheerleader throughout this incredible journey. You are my "Perfect Fit!"

Audrey, you are the love of my life, the one who brings joy to every moment we share. From our travels around the world to the quiet nights spent experimenting with new cocktail creations, you have been by my side, infusing every experience with your warmth and love.

Not only have you supported my passion for being a great leader, but you have also effortlessly juggled the responsibilities of our lives, always putting others before yourself. Your unwavering dedication and tireless efforts have made it possible for me to pursue my dreams with boundless enthusiasm.

You are not only my loving wife but also my agent, guiding me through the intricacies of the publishing world. Your insights, wisdom, and unwavering belief in my abilities have propelled me forward, pushing me to reach new heights.

Above all, Audrey, you are my best friend. We have laughed, cried, and celebrated together, creating memories that will last a lifetime. Your love and support have been the foundation on which I built this book, and I am forever grateful for your presence in my life.

So, with heartfelt gratitude and immeasurable love, I dedicate "Leadership Mastery: Unlock Your Full Potential and Lead With Impact" to you, Audrey D. Mullins. May this book serve as a testament to the remarkable woman you are and the profound impact you have had on my journey as an author and leader.

Cheers to you, my love, and to the perfect purpose of our lives together.

With all my love,

Dennis

Prologue

In "Leadership Mastery: Unlock Your Full Potential and Lead with Impact," readers will embark on a transformative journey towards becoming exceptional leaders. This comprehensive guide addresses the most pressing questions, problems, fears, frustrations, and challenges faced by management and leadership professionals.

The book begins with an introduction that emphasizes the importance of leadership development and highlights how the content will benefit readers. Each chapter is strategically designed to provide practical insights, actionable strategies, and real-world examples to facilitate growth and development.

TABLE OF CONTENTS

Becoming an effective leader 1

Strategies for Improving Management Skills 7

Inspiring and Motivating Your Team 10

Key Principles of Successful Leadership................13

Navigating Challenging Business Situations 16

Best Practices for Negotiation and Persuasion 36

Enhancing Strategic Thinking and Decision-Making Abilities 40

Secrets to Building High-Performing Teams.........47

Effective Time and Priority Management 51

Training Exercises...57

Becoming an effective leader

Becoming an effective leader requires cultivating self-awareness, emotional intelligence, strong communication skills, and an ability to inspire trust and credibility. Influential leaders embrace various leadership styles while continuously developing themselves with integrity and ethics in mind. Successful leaders gain a comprehensive knowledge of themselves, their team, and their organization, which allows them to make informed decisions, motivate others, and drive organizational success - mastering these key components will enable individuals to become powerful influencers who bring positive change while producing remarkable results.

Becoming an effective leader can be an intricate journey requiring many skills and qualities. Let's dive deeper into each suggested strategy and look at real-life examples of how they could be implemented.

1. Self-awareness: Great leaders understand their strengths, weaknesses, values, and beliefs as a foundation of continuous development. For instance, Steve Jobs of Apple fame was well known for his self-awareness - acknowledging his perfectionist tendencies while harnessing them productively towards developing innovative and groundbreaking products.

2. Emotional Intelligence: Effective leaders possess emotional intelligence. Howard Schultz, former CEO of Starbucks and an outstanding example of emotional intelligence, understood the significance of creating a positive and inclusive work environment, contributing to Starbucks' success and expansion.

3. Strong Communication Skills: Leaders need effective communication skills that allow them to articulate their vision, goals, and expectations effectively while actively listening and providing constructive feedback. Indra Nooyi of PepsiCo demonstrated exceptional communication abilities by encouraging open and honest communications within her organization, encouraging collaboration and innovation.

4. Fostering Trust and Credibility: Trust is essential for effective leadership. Trustworthy leaders act with integrity, fulfill commitments, and are transparent about their actions. Satya Nadella, the CEO of Microsoft, has achieved success at inspiring trust by adopting a growth mindset while creating an inclusive culture that promotes innovation and creativity.

5. Recognizing and Acknowledging Different Leadership Styles: Effective leaders understand and accept varying leadership styles. Mary Barra, CEO of General Motors, is well known for balancing her collaborative leadership approach with making tough decisions when necessary. This flexibility has allowed her to lead General Motors through tough times successfully.

6. Continuous Self-Development: Great leaders prioritize personal growth and development. They seek learning opportunities, stay current on industry trends, and encourage team members to do the same. Jeff Bezos, founder and former CEO of Amazon, is an example of someone who practices continuous self-development; his commitment to innovation and willingness to take risks has helped propel it to become one of the world's most valuable businesses.

7. Leading with Integrity and Ethics: Ethical leaders prioritize doing what is right even in challenging circumstances, setting an example, and holding themselves and others accountable. Ellen Kullman, former CEO of DuPont, demonstrated ethical leadership by prioritizing sustainability and safety and making responsible

business decisions that were good for both her company and the environment.

By implementing these strategies and learning from successful leaders' examples, individuals can develop into impactful leaders capable of driving positive change and producing impressive results. Remember that leadership is an ongoing journey of growth and adaptation!

Unleashing Your Inner Strength Through Leadership

Leadership is the cornerstone of unlocking the potential within individuals, teams, and organizations. As a multifaceted concept encompassing skills, traits, and behaviors ranging from skillsets and traits to behaviors, its definition provides us with essential principles underpinning effective leadership - emotional intelligence is important in developing practical strategies for leading with impactful leadership styles.

Definition of Leadership

For an accurate understanding of leadership, it is necessary to define it properly. At its core, leadership refers to the art of leading individuals and teams towards a common goal - not simply as an employment title or position but as a mindset and set of behaviors that inspire and influence other people. A leader is someone who possesses the ability to inspire trust while communicating clearly, making informed decisions quickly, managing challenges with grace and resilience, and leading through them with resilience.

Principles of Effective Leadership

Now that we understand what leadership is, let's delve into its principles:

1. Self-awareness: Self-awareness is at the core of effective leadership. This involves understanding one's own strengths, weaknesses, values, and emotions - helping leaders align their actions with core values while making conscious choices that reflect authentic selves.

2. Self-Regulation: Emotional intelligence is an integral component of successful leadership, as it requires one to recognize and control their emotions in challenging situations. Leaders who possess this skill are better able to maintain composure, make rational decisions, and deal with adversity more successfully.

3. Motivation: Successful leaders possess a deep sense of purpose and passion for what they do, inspiring and motivating others with their enthusiasm and dedication. By setting clear goals, giving meaningful feedback, and creating an inspiring work environment, leaders can spark intrinsic motivation among their teams.

4. Empathy: Empathy allows leaders to connect more closely with their team members on an emotional level and build meaningful relationships based on trust and mutual respect. Demonstrating empathy enables leaders to foster an environment in which each employee feels appreciated and respected - creating an inclusive working environment where individuals feel understood.

5. Social Skills: Exemplary leaders possess strong interpersonal communication and relationship-building abilities that allow them to collaborate, negotiate and resolve conflict effectively. By encouraging open and transparent communication channels between teams and leaders, effective leaders can foster an environment conducive to trust, collaboration, and innovation within an organization.

Implementing Emotional Intelligence for Leadership Success

Enhancing emotional intelligence is a lifelong pursuit that involves self-reflection, practice, and ongoing learning. If you want to develop emotional intelligence as a leader, here are a few strategies:

1. Increase self-awareness through self-reflection, journaling, and seeking feedback from others. Understand your strengths, weaknesses, and triggers while working toward aligning your actions with your values.

2. Develop effective self-regulation by understanding and managing your emotions. Employ techniques like deep breathing, mindfulness, and positive self-talk to stay centered during stressful moments.

3. Strive to understand others by actively listening and showing empathy, placing yourself in their shoes, and trying to see things from their perspective. Establish strong relationships by showing genuine interest and support.

4. Enhance your social skills by sharpening your communication and negotiation abilities. Engage in active listening, assertiveness training, conflict resolution methods, and conflict prevention measures - creating an atmosphere where honest discussions are welcomed by others.

5. Be proactive about learning and growing by seeking feedback, attending leadership development programs, reading books on emotional intelligence and leadership, and seeking out mentors or role models who exemplify the qualities you admire.

Leadership is a complex concept that demands an in-depth knowledge of oneself and others. Emotional intelligence plays a central role in effective leadership, helping leaders to motivate, inspire, and guide their teams toward success. By adhering to principles such as self-awareness, self-regulation, motivation, empathy, and social skills, leaders can unlock their full potential and have a lasting positive effect on those they lead. Remember: leadership isn't simply a position; rather, it is an ongoing journey of self-discovery, growth, and transformation, which can become catalysts of positive change within organizations and communities alike.

Strategies for Improving Management Skills

As part of becoming an effective leader, developing strong management skills is crucial. These include setting clear goals and expectations while building high-performing teams. In this chapter, we'll look at strategies and techniques that can help managers enhance their management abilities. Mastering these can create an efficient work environment, meet organizational objectives, and motivate teams toward excellence.

Management's Role in Leadership

Management plays a critical role in leadership. It involves overseeing daily operations, leading a team toward goals, and making sure tasks are completed efficiently. Effective managers understand the importance of striking a balance between meeting organizational requirements and meeting team member needs, as well as providing guidance, support, and resources so their teams can perform at their maximum capacity.

Setting Clear Goals and Expectations

One of the key duties of any manager is setting clear goals and expectations for their team. Goals provide direction and ensure everyone works towards one common objective. Managers should communicate these goals effectively so all team members understand their roles, responsibilities, and expected outcomes.

Enhance Your Planning and Organization Skills

Managers rely heavily on effective planning and organizational skills for success in their roles. Successful managers possessing these abilities should prioritize tasks, allocate resources efficiently, create action plans to achieve goals, optimize productivity, and ensure tasks are completed on schedule. By planning and organizing effectively, managers can improve productivity while managing time efficiently and making sure tasks get accomplished on schedule.

Delegating Tasks and Empowering Others

Delegation is a key skill for managers to acquire. By assigning tasks to team members, managers can empower their team members, foster professional growth, and increase productivity. Effective delegation requires assigning tasks based on individuals' individual strengths and abilities as well as providing clear instructions with support available when needed. Managers should give team members autonomy in making decisions that contribute to team success.

Building and Leading High-Performing Teams

Building and leading an exceptional team requires managers to possess essential management skills. Managers should aim at recruiting individuals with appropriate skills and attitudes, creating a positive team culture, encouraging collaboration and open communication, regularly providing feedback, rewarding achievements, and addressing any conflicts or challenges within their team by providing this supportive and inclusive environment for their team members to thrive and realize their full potential resulting in exceptional results.

Effective Decision-Making Techniques

Managers often face the task of making important decisions that could have long-term effects on their organization and team members. Effective decision-making requires gathering relevant information, taking multiple perspectives into account, and weighing potential outcomes against each other. Managers can utilize techniques like SWOT analysis, brainstorming, or weighing pros and cons when making informed decisions; furthermore, they must be open to feedback and willing to alter them when necessary.

Problem Solving and Critical Thinking Skills

Problem-solving and critical thinking abilities are critical tools for managers who wish to meet challenges head-on and find innovative solutions. To effectively approach any challenge with innovative ideas, managers should approach problems systematically and analytically, identify root causes, and consider alternative solutions before inviting team members in on problem-solving processes and encouraging continuous improvement processes among them.

Continuous Learning and Adaptability

Managers must adopt a mindset of constant learning and adaptability in order to remain effective leaders. By continuously seeking opportunities for professional growth and attending training programs, as well as keeping up with industry trends and best practices, managers can enhance their management skills, stay ahead of competitors, and effectively navigate changes and challenges presented in today's business environments.

Improving management skills is crucial to effective leadership. By employing strategies such as setting clear goals, developing planning and organizational skills, delegating tasks, building and managing high-performing teams, employing effective decision-making techniques, developing problem-solving and critical thinking abilities, and accepting continual learning and adaptability as means to do this, managers can enhance their effectiveness and foster a positive and productive work environment for themselves and their teams alike. By mastering these abilities, they can lead their teams toward success, meet organizational objectives, and foster growth and innovation within their organizations.

Inspiring and Motivating Your Team

One of your main duties as a leader is inspiring and motivating your team members to reach their full potential. By creating a positive work environment, providing meaningful feedback, cultivating a culture of collaboration, and leading by example, you can spark motivation within team members. In this chapter, we will examine strategies and principles that will enable you to inspire and motivate them toward excellence.

Understanding Motivation and its Implications on Performance

Motivation is at the core of individual and team performance. Understanding what motivates your team members is vital for effectively inspiring and motivating them; different individuals may be driven by different things such as recognition, personal growth, or a sense of purpose; by understanding these motivations, you can tailor your leadership approach and foster an environment that supports high performance and engagement.

Create an Engaging Work Environment

An engaging work environment is the key to motivating and inspiring your team. Instill a culture of respect, trust, and open communication in order to foster collaboration and teamwork as well as provide opportunities for personal and professional growth. Foster a supportive atmosphere where members feel valued, appreciated, and motivated to provide their best work.

Provide Meaningful Feedback and Recognition

Meaningful feedback and recognition play an integral role in motivating and inspiring team members. Provide regular, constructive feedback highlighting areas for improvement as well as strengths. Recognize and celebrate achievements - large or small! Show genuine gratitude for efforts put forth; this will not only increase motivation but reinforce positive behaviors and performance as well.

Coaching and Mentoring to Accelerate Growth.

Coaching and mentoring are effective tools for inspiring and motivating team members. Taking an active interest in their professional growth and offering guidance and support to achieve their goals, as well as skill-building opportunities and constructive guidance when facing challenges, coaching, and mentoring, will inspire team members to take ownership over their development and strive for excellence.

Fostering Collaboration and Teamwork at Work

Collaboration and teamwork are integral parts of an efficient and motivated team. Foster a culture where team members feel at ease sharing ideas, collaborating on projects, supporting one another, encouraging open communication, and creating opportunities for cross-functional collaboration - this will encourage your members to work towards shared goals while producing remarkable results!

Empowering Employees and Inducing Ownership at Work

Empowering employees and encouraging ownership are two essential elements of motivation. Grant your team members autonomy to make decisions and take ownership of their work. Delegate tasks and responsibilities tailored to their skill set. Encourage initiative, innovation, and challenge-taking as ways of driving motivation. Doing this will foster increased motivation and engagement in your workforce.

Leading by Example and Motivating Others

Your actions as a leader speak louder than words. Lead by example and show the behaviors and values you expect of your team - including integrity, resilience, strong work ethic, and transparency in communication. Inspire others through your actions and inspire them to follow in your footsteps - your enthusiasm and dedication will motivate and encourage your team members to give their best efforts!

Building a Shared Vision and Purpose

Build a shared vision and purpose to engage and motivate your team members. Communicate the organization's mission and objectives, linking them directly with team goals. Help team members see how their work contributes to the bigger picture of the organization's success; by aligning individual goals with this shared vision, you will foster an atmosphere of purposefulness and dedication among team members.

Motivating and inspiring your team is essential to effective leadership. Understanding motivation, creating a positive work environment, providing meaningful feedback, coaching and mentoring employees, leading by example, and creating a shared vision can all play an essential part. With these strategies in place, your leadership will inspire team members to go above and beyond in achieving outstanding results for your organization's overall success.

Key Principles of Successful Leadership

Successful leadership involves inspiring and empowering others to realize their full potential. In this chapter, we'll explore some key principles underlying effective leadership - from visionary leadership that creates compelling future visions to ethical decision-making with integrity - all designed to make you an effective and impactful leader.

Visionary Leadership: Envisioning an Engaging Future

Visionary leadership involves creating a compelling vision of the future that inspires and motivates others, providing direction for action. A visionary leader effectively communicates this vision, uniting team members toward one common goal while invigorating them toward its accomplishment.

Transformational Leadership: Empowering and Develop Others

Transformational leadership emphasizes empowering and developing others. A transformational leader achieves this through creating strong relationships, inspiring trust, creating an enabling environment, and helping team members realize their full potential. They provide guidance, mentorship, and support, encouraging both personal and professional growth among their team members. Their style of leadership encourages collaboration and innovation, resulting in higher levels of engagement and performance for everyone on their team. Transformational leadership stands in sharp contrast to transactional, which relies heavily on bureaucratic authority. Transactional leaders focus mainly on task completion and employee compliance, while more successful leaders pursue transformational approaches with an eye toward team empowerment and development.

Servant Leadership: Placing Others First

Servant leadership entails prioritizing others before oneself. A servant leader prioritizes understanding and supporting team members' needs while actively listening, showing empathy, and encouraging team growth and well-being. By doing this, a servant leader fosters an environment of trust, respect, collaboration, and an engaged workforce - qualities essential for effective servant leadership.

Adaptive Leadership: Navigating Change and Uncertainty

Adaptive leadership is key for effectively handling change and uncertainty. A leader who adheres to this principle should be flexible, open-minded, and agile when approaching issues and transitions affecting their team while being mindful of external environmental shifts affecting them and providing guidance through them. An Adaptive leader fosters innovation while cultivating a learning mindset for their staff so they can embrace change rapidly and adjust quickly as the situation requires.

Authentic Leadership: Leading with Purpose and Values

Authentic leadership involves leading with genuine purpose and values in mind. An Authentic leader embodies their own beliefs while showing their integrity through the actions they take - they inspire trust through honesty and consistency, creating an environment in which team members feel safe, respected, and inspired to perform at their best.

Resilient Leadership: Thriving Under Pressure

Resilient leadership is vital to success in today's uncertain business environment. A resilient leader remains composed and adaptive during difficult periods, providing their team with confidence and optimism. They accept failure as a learning opportunity while encouraging others in their team to do the same. Through showing resilience, leaders create an atmosphere of perseverance, innovation, and continuous improvement within their organization.

Inclusive Leadership: Promoting Diversity and Inclusion

Inclusive leadership involves welcoming diversity and cultivating an inclusive culture. An inclusive leader recognizes and appreciates all perspectives and contributions made by their team members, creating an atmosphere in which everyone feels respected, heard, and valued. Leveraging their diverse team's strengths to drive innovation, collaboration, and high performance.

Ethical Leadership: Making Decisions with Integrity

Ethical leadership involves making decisions with integrity while upholding high ethical standards and acting according to their values. An ethical leader prioritizes doing what is right even in challenging circumstances by upholding ethical behavior and decision-making and encouraging an environment of honesty and accountability among their team and stakeholders. Successful leadership requires continuous growth and development - let's explore each principle's contribution toward effective leadership together!

The key principles of successful leadership provide a roadmap for becoming an impactful and efficient leader. Adopting visionary, transformational, servant, adaptive, authentic, resilient, and inclusive leadership ethics as your guideposts for becoming an impactful leader who not only produces excellent results but leaves lasting impressions with individuals and organizations you lead. By adopting these principles as your compass, you will create an inspiring work environment for both team members and clients while successfully managing challenging circumstances and creating high-performing work environments for success.

Navigating Challenging Business Situations

Leaders on every business journey face unexpected obstacles and difficulties; to successfully overcome them, leaders require both skills and mindset that allow them to overcome these difficulties successfully. In this chapter, we will explore key principles and strategies for successfully navigating difficult business situations - understanding their dynamics, building a resilient mindset, problem-solving strategies that work, managing conflict sensitively in conversations, leading through change and uncertainty effectively, crisis management decision-making abilities in challenging circumstances, as well as learning from failure and turning setbacks into opportunities.

Understanding Business Challenges

In order to navigate difficult business situations successfully, leaders must first gain an in-depth knowledge of their dynamics. Leaders should identify the root causes of the challenges as well as evaluate potential repercussions for the organization. Through comprehensive assessment processes, leaders can develop an accurate picture of what challenges their organizations are currently facing and make well-informed decisions.

Resilience is key to meeting challenges head-on, so leaders must cultivate a resilient mindset to tackle problems successfully. They should view failure as an opportunity to learn something new and view challenges as stepping stones on their journey to growth. By increasing resilience among their teams and themselves, leaders can inspire perseverance and innovation within their organization.

Effective Problem-Solving Strategies

Successful problem-solving is essential when facing challenging business situations, so leaders should approach issues systematically and analytically. They should gather relevant data, consult key stakeholders, brainstorm potential solutions, and evaluate all available options so as to make informed decisions and implement lasting solutions. Effective problem-solving is a fundamental skill of leadership - here are a few approaches they can employ for effective problem-solving.

1. Define the Issue: Accurately identify your issue or challenge, taking time to understand its root cause and identify any specific concerns or needs that need addressing. By accurately defining it, your efforts can be directed toward finding effective solutions.

2. Assessing the Situation: Gather all relevant information and assess it from various perspectives, breaking down the problem into smaller components to investigate individually and seek patterns, trends, causes, or potential effects that impact various stakeholders - this step will give you a deeper insight into its source and help identify possible solutions to it.

3. Generate Alternative Solutions: Brainstorm and generate alternative solutions through brainstorming sessions. Avoid being convinced by just one idea that comes to mind; encourage diverse perspectives and involve team members or stakeholders as part of this process. Consider both traditional and innovative approaches; ultimately, your aim should be to generate multiple potential solutions that can later be evaluated for viability.

4. Evaluate Options and Reach a Decision: Evaluate each alternative solution carefully in terms of pros and cons, feasibility, potential risks, and benefits before reaching a decision based on all available information. When reviewing options, use criteria that align with your organization's goals and values to assess them; seek input from relevant stakeholders or subject matter experts

when necessary to assess them thoroughly before reaching your conclusion based on all available information.

5. Implement and Monitor: Create an action plan to implement the chosen solution, identify any necessary resources, assign responsibilities, and set clear timelines. Communicate this plan to stakeholders for their buy-in before monitoring progress as you implement your chosen solution and adjusting as necessary as you go along. Continually assess effectiveness and solicit feedback as it's implemented to ensure continuous improvement.

Effective problem-solving requires learning from errors and changing approaches over time, creating an environment of continuous improvement with feedback from teammates and stakeholders alike. Through employing these problem-solving strategies, leaders can successfully navigate challenges within their organizations while driving positive transformation.

Conflict and Difficult Conversations

Difficult and challenging conversations are inevitable in difficult business situations, so leaders need to possess strong interpersonal skills in order to manage them effectively. Leaders should foster open communication, active listening, and empathy as a means of managing these challenging discussions effectively and reaching resolutions while building positive working relationships with employees. Navigating conflicts directly and constructively is an invaluable skill for new leaders. Here are five effective approaches new leaders can employ in handling conflict and difficult discussions.

1. Prepare and Plan: Before engaging in any difficult conversation or addressing a conflict, take the time to plan in advance. Set clear objectives, gather relevant information, consider different perspectives, anticipate possible obstacles that could arise, and plan a way forward - this preparation will enable you to approach the conversation with clarity and confidence.

2. Cultivate a Safe and Respectful Environment: Create an atmosphere in which all parties involved feel free to express their thoughts and concerns without feeling judged or threatened by another. Emphasize active listening, facilitate open dialogue, set ground rules for discussions such as speaking respectfully while inviting all views to share their perspective on issues at hand, as well as focus on finding solutions.

3. Focus on Understanding: Instead of immediately trying to come up with solutions or defend your position, seek to understand all aspects and perspectives involved. Ask open-ended questions, listen actively, and seek to understand emotions or concerns behind their viewpoints - this empathetic approach may help de-escalate conflicts while building the groundwork for creating common ground.

4. Practice Effective Communication: Use clear and direct language to express your thoughts and express any issues or concerns. Be conscious of your tone and body language as they can sway the course of a conversation, use "I" statements instead of blaming or accusatory language when expressing feelings, and never condemn others for sharing their viewpoints freely. Embark upon constructive feedback sessions while encouraging others to express themselves.

5. Collaborate and Find Solutions: Instead of approaching conflict as a zero-sum game, aim for a collaborative solution by working together towards finding mutually beneficial solutions. Prioritize shared goals and interests when considering possible resolution options and encourage brainstorming sessions as part of creative problem-solving efforts. Be open to compromise as well as exploring different perspectives.

After your conversation, it is key to follow up in order to ensure any agreements or action plans made are implemented and monitored accordingly. Check-in regularly with all parties involved so you can evaluate progress and address any ongoing concerns.

Be mindful that managing conflict and difficult conversations is an ongoing learning experience. Seek feedback, reflect upon your experiences, and continually enhance your approach as a means of developing the necessary skills necessary for successfully handling these discussions. With such skills in hand, new leaders can effectively navigate conflict management processes for positive and productive work environments.

Leading Through Change and Uncertainty

Leaders must master leading their teams through change and uncertainty with ease in business environments, providing support and resources, and encouraging a growth mindset - leaders can inspire their teams to adapt and thrive under challenging situations by accepting change as it arises and engaging their staff in accepting it as well. Effective team leaders require certain skills and strategies; here are some ways that new leaders can develop these abilities for leading teams through transformation.

1. Gain an Understanding of the Change Process: Educate yourself on the different stages of the change process, such as denial, resistance, exploration, and commitment. Become acquainted with change management models and theories to gain an in-depth knowledge of how individuals and teams adapt to change.

2. Communicate Effectively: Open and timely communication is of utmost importance in times of change and uncertainty. Develop strong communication skills to clearly explain the reasons for change, its anticipated effects, and your vision for its future impact. Be open and accessible for feedback from team members during times of transition.

3. Build a Supportive Culture: Establish an environment in which team members feel safe expressing their concerns, asking

questions, and sharing ideas. Engage in open dialogue and active listening sessions in order to mitigate fears or resistance during times of change.

4. Provide Clarity and Direction: Articulate the goals and objectives of the change initiative with clarity. Clearly set realistic expectations with your team members. Break the change process down into smaller steps so that all team members understand their roles and responsibilities more readily.

5. Empower and Engage Team Members: Enable your team members to actively participate in the change process by including them in decision-making, seeking their input, and encouraging them to take ownership of their work. Doing this not only increases engagement but also builds trust and commitment towards it.

6. Build Resilience: Leading through change is often challenging and stressful, so building resilience to help effectively handle uncertainty and setbacks is essential to effectively leading through transformation. Practicing self-care, maintaining a positive outlook, and seeking support from mentors or colleagues experienced with leading change can all be useful strategies for managing it.

7. Lead by Example: Be an example to your team by showing adaptability, flexibility, and an upbeat outlook towards change. Show them that you embrace uncertainty while remaining resilient, as this will inspire and motivate them to do the same.

8. Provide Training and Development Opportunities: Invest in yourself professionally by seeking opportunities to expand your change management abilities. Attend workshops, seminars, or courses focused on leading through change. Share your knowledge and provide training opportunities for your team so they may develop their own change management abilities.

9. Lear from Experience: Evaluate past experiences leading your team through change and identify what worked well and where improvements could have been made. Use this insight to enhance your approach and formulate strategies that will enable your team to adapt smoothly to future changes.

10. Seek Feedback and Learn From Others: Ensure your team and other leaders who have successfully navigated through change provide regular feedback so you can learn from their experiences, best practices, and lessons learned. Networking and developing relationships with other leaders may offer invaluable support and insights.

Implementing these strategies allows new leaders to develop the necessary skills needed to lead their team successfully through change and uncertainty. Effective communication, creating a supportive culture, engaging team members in decision-making processes, and continuously learning and adapting are essential parts of leading teams through change successfully.

Crisis Management and Decision-Making

Leaders must respond swiftly and decisively during times of crisis, setting clear protocols and communication channels in place to handle it efficiently. Based on available information and seeking input from relevant stakeholders, informed decisions must be made that demonstrate calmness and confidence to lead their teams through crises without negatively affecting the organization. Here are some strategies for developing crisis management skills:

1. Construct a Crisis Management Plan: Establish an in-depth crisis management plan outlining what steps should be taken during any potential crises. Identify possible crisis scenarios, assess risks, and create clear protocols and procedures for response. Assign roles and responsibilities to team members for optimal coordination during an incident.

2. Conduct Risk Evaluations: Perform regular risk evaluations within your organization in order to identify any risks and vulnerabilities within. Doing this proactively allows leaders to recognize potential crisis triggers and implement preventative measures; anticipating crises allows leaders to respond more quickly when they arise.

3. Strengthen Communication Skills: Effective communication during a crisis is absolutely critical, so leaders should develop strong communication skills that allow them to relay key information clearly and promptly to all relevant parties, including employees, customers, partners, media members, etc. Transparency, accuracy, and consistency are keys to maintaining trust while effectively managing a crisis situation.

4. Establish a Crisis Response Team: Bring together a group of individuals with various talents and expertise in order to address crisis situations effectively and quickly. Delegate specific roles and responsibilities among team members; conduct regular training and simulation exercises in order to make sure your response team can react swiftly and efficiently during an emergency.

5. Practice Decisive Decision-Making Under Pressure: Emergencies often necessitate quick and decisive decision-making under pressure, so new leaders should practice making well-informed decisions efficiently to mitigate potential negative repercussions in emergency situations.

6. Stay Calm and Composed: Leaders must remain calm and collected during times of crisis, as panic or uncertainty can exacerbate a situation and prevent effective decision-making. Projecting confidence and stability helps build confidence in others while creating a sense of stability during challenging periods.

7. Collaborate and Delegate: Crisis management requires collaboration from all members of a team, drawing upon each person's expertise and perspectives to best manage crises.

Delegating tasks and responsibilities accordingly allows leaders to focus on critical decision-making as part of an overall crisis management strategy.

8. Learn from Past Crises: Consider past crisis situations to reflect and gain from them, analyzing what worked well and where improvement could be made. Conduct post-crisis evaluations to identify areas for improvement and update the crisis management plan accordingly. By constantly learning from experience and adapting accordingly, your crisis management skills can only grow stronger over time.

9. Build Resilience: Crisis situations can be emotionally and mentally taxing on leaders, so they should build resilience to cope with stress and uncertainty. Doing this involves practicing self-care, seeking support from colleagues and mentors, and keeping an optimistic perspective.

10. Engage in Continuous Learning: Stay abreast of best practices and emerging trends in crisis management by attending workshops, seminars, and conferences related to it and engaging in professional development activities that expand your knowledge in this area.

By following these strategies, new leaders can develop strong crisis management skills and successfully navigate challenging situations. Being prepared, communicating clearly, making informed decisions, and learning from experience are essential elements of becoming a successful crisis manager.

Influencing and Negotiation Skills in Challenging Situations

Leaders facing difficult business scenarios require strong influencing and negotiation skills. They must build rapport, communicate persuasively, and seek win-win solutions with stakeholders while respecting their motivations and interests when tailoring their approach accordingly. By effectively using influence and negotiation to overcome obstacles and secure positive outcomes for all, effective leadership is possible.

Establishing strong negotiation skills is essential for new leaders to effectively navigate business situations. Here are some strategies to hone these essential capabilities.

1. Assess the Situation: Begin your negotiation by fully comprehending its context and dynamics, such as identifying interests, needs, motivations, and potential roadblocks among parties involved. Conduct research and gather relevant information that supports your position while anticipating potential challenges that might arise from it.

2. Prepare Thoroughly: Before entering any negotiation, prioritize preparation by outlining your goals, objectives, and desired outcomes, as well as developing an accurate understanding of both parties' strengths and weaknesses. Anticipate potential objections or counterarguments and prepare convincing replies.

3. Build Rapport: Forming positive relationships is paramount to effective negotiation. Do this by actively listening, showing empathy, and showing genuine interest in their perspective - these methods will create a trust that fosters more collaborative negotiation environments.

4. Engage in Active Listening: Effective negotiations require attentive listening skills. Pay careful attention to what the other party says in terms of words, body language, and underlying interests - this will allow you to better comprehend their needs, concerns, and priorities, as well as demonstrate your attentiveness by asking clarifying questions about what was said earlier - this also serves to build rapport!

5. Focus on Win-Win Solutions: When engaging in negotiations, aim for mutually beneficial results that benefit both parties involved. Try finding creative solutions to meet both sides'

interests and needs; by treating negotiations as a problem-solving activity, you can explore options that add maximum value for all sides while strengthening long-term relationships.

6. Leverage Effective Communication: Make your position, needs, and expectations clear during negotiations by using concise yet persuasive language to present them. Be conscious of your tone and body language as they can influence negotiation dynamics; aim for common ground among parties involved while closing any communication gaps that exist between you and other participants.

7. Be Flexible and Open-Minded: Effective negotiators are open-minded when it comes to finding alternative solutions. Be willing to explore various avenues and perspectives when making decisions and accept compromise when it serves your overall goals and objectives.

8. Manage Your Emotions: Maintain composure during negotiations by remaining composed and professional at all times, even in challenging situations. Anger or passion can cloud judgment and inhibit effective decision-making; if tensions flare during an argumentative negotiation session, take a break or arrange to meet later so cooler heads can prevail.

9. Demonstrate Confidence: Exude confidence in yourself, your negotiation abilities, and the value you bring to the table. Displaying confidence can positively influence perceptions of you as credible and strengthen your position; just be wary not to become arrogant or too aggressive, as this could damage relationships.

10. Learn from Experience: Review each negotiation experience to identify areas for improvement, consider what went well and where you could have handled things differently, seek feedback from colleagues or mentors with expertise in negotiation, refine your skills through practice and learning from both successes and failures, then keep practicing and refining them over time.

By following these strategies, new leaders can develop strong negotiation skills that enable them to effectively advocate for their interests while building relationships and reaching mutually beneficial outcomes.

Learning From Failure and Turning Setbacks Into Opportunities

Failure and setbacks provide valuable learning experiences. Leaders should foster a culture in which failure is seen as an opportunity for personal and professional growth by analyzing past failures, identifying lessons learned, and making necessary improvements. Failure is essential to personal and professional growth for new leaders alike - here are some ways these emerging leaders can use failure as a valuable learning experience:

1. Adopt a Growth Mindset: Adopt a mindset that views failure as part of the learning process and an opportunity for progress rather than an indication of personal failure. Failure is inevitable but shouldn't be seen as evidence against us or cause for disappointment.

2. Analyze the Failure: Reflect back on what went wrong, identify any specific decisions or factors that contributed to its occurrence, as well as consider both internal factors (like skills, knowledge, or decision-making abilities) as well as external ones, such as unforeseeable circumstances or market conditions (i.e., market conditions).

3. Take Ownership: Admitting responsibility for failure allows you to focus on learning from it and finding solutions instead of dwelling on past errors. Acknowledge your role in its creation is key, as well as being accountable for all actions taken during its completion.

4. Seek Feedback: Get feedback from trusted mentors, colleagues, or team members who can offer objective insights. Seek their input

regarding what could have been done differently or lessons to be learned - don't be defensive when receiving constructive criticism; use it to improve future actions!

5. Extract Key Learnings: Examine what lessons or insights can be gleaned from failure, including its influence on decision-making, problem-solving, or leadership practices in future situations and potential lessons applicable across situations similar to your failure.

6. Adapt and Adjust: Take the learnings from failure as opportunities to adapt and refine your strategies or approaches in future endeavors or incorporate insights gained into decision-making processes and future actions. Create a continuous improvement mindset where failure becomes an opportunity for growth and refinement.

7. Share Your Experiences: Sharing your failure experience and its lessons learned with your team or colleagues fosters an environment in which failures are seen as opportunities for growth, as well as showing authenticity as a leader. This also demonstrates vulnerability.

8. Encourage Risk-Taking: Foster an environment that embraces calculated risk-taking and experimentation. Urge your team members to move out of their comfort zones, experiment, learn from failure, and celebrate efforts over avoiding failure.

Accepting failure as an opportunity for growth, new leaders can hone resilience, adaptability, and a growth mindset. Learning from failures may lead to better decision-making processes, innovative problem-solving techniques, and long-term success.

Navigating Challenging Business Situations

Navigating challenging business situations can be a complex and time-consuming task for leaders, requiring a combination of skills, mindset, and strategies in order to overcome obstacles effectively and find success. To address challenges effectively, leaders need to have an in-depth knowledge of the dynamics at play - including root causes of challenges as well as impact assessments within an organization and gaining insights into the broader context. By understanding this dynamic effectively, leaders can devise tailored plans of attack against challenges effectively and address these effectively.

Recognizing the source of any difficult situation is key for new leaders looking to address issues effectively and prevent their recurrence. Here are some strategies designed to assist new leaders with this endeavor:

1. Gather Information: Start by gathering pertinent information about the challenging situation. Consult team members, stakeholders, and any individuals directly involved to gain different perspectives on it. Additionally, collect any pertinent data, reports, or documentation that might shed some light on how best to approach it.

2. Pose Questions: Attempt to ask probing questions that explore the underlying factors affecting a situation, encourage open and honest communication, and create an atmosphere in which individuals feel safe to express their views and share concerns freely. Be curious and pose inquiries that inquire into the context, processes, and motivations involved.

3. Conduct Root Cause Analysis: Utilizing techniques such as "5 Whys" or fishbone diagrams can be used to systematically identify underlying causes. Ask "why" questions regularly until you uncover its core. Analyze factors, including processes, systems, communication channels, resources, and external influences, when conducting this analysis.

4. Apply Data and Metrics: Use data and metrics to gain objective insight into any situation, analyzing performance indicators, trends,

patterns, and correlations to spot any correlations or causality that might exist between events or causes and results. Ultimately, data-driven decision-making provides more accurate root cause identification as well as providing a basis for efficient problem-solving solutions.

5. Seek Diverse Perspectives: Seeking diverse viewpoints requires engaging individuals from various departments, backgrounds, and expertise - engaging these can provide a holistic overview of a situation while uncovering factors that have been overlooked or dismissed outright. Foster brainstorming sessions, as this helps generate innovative solutions.

6. Promote Feedback and Reflection: Foster an environment in which individuals feel comfortable providing feedback and reflecting upon their own actions, with self-assessment and continuous improvement being encouraged throughout. Nurture an atmosphere where mistakes can be seen as opportunities to grow professionally.

7. Consider External Factors: Understand any outside influences that could be contributing to a challenging situation, such as market conditions, industry trends, regulatory changes, or economic forces that are beyond your team or organization's control. Analyzing the external landscape can help identify root causes outside its realm.

8. Engage Relevant Stakeholders: Seek input from all those with expertise or influence who could potentially make an effective contribution to solving this challenging situation. Be open-minded when asking their advice - their knowledge can provide great insight into what could be driving this problem at its source.

9. Continuous Improvement: Implement a culture of continuous improvement where root cause analysis becomes part of daily work activities. Encourage team members to proactively identify and address potential issues before they escalate further while

periodically reviewing processes, systems, and practices to pinpoint areas for enhancement.

Implementing these strategies allows new leaders to effectively pinpoint the source of challenging situations and take measures to resolve them, leading to long-term solutions and preventing similar issues from recurring in the future.

Resilience is crucial when facing challenges.

Leaders must foster an environment that embraces adversity as an opportunity for growth and view setbacks as learning experiences for their teams. By developing resilience, leaders can foster innovation, perseverance, and adaptability among their workforce.

Establishing a resilient culture is crucial for new leaders who wish to effectively lead their teams through challenges and foster growth. Here are some ways to foster one:

1. Lead by Example: As a leader, show resilience by remaining calm, composed, and optimistic during times of adversity. Show your team that setbacks or failures provide opportunities for learning and personal development.

2. Foster Open Communication: Encourage open and transparent communication within your team by creating a safe space where team members can voice their concerns, share ideas, or ask for support. Actively listen to their viewpoints while offering constructive advice as necessary.

3. Establish Clear Goals and Expectations: Clearly define goals and expectations to provide direction and purpose to team members' work while making sure it contributes to the larger vision of your organization. Break larger goals down into manageable milestones to foster progress and a sense of achievement.

4. Welcome Change and Adaptability: Help your team accept change by emphasizing the importance of flexibility and adaptability. Remind them to see it as an opportunity for growth and innovation rather than as a threat, providing all resources and support necessary for smooth transitions.

5. Foster Learning and Development: Promote an environment of continual learning and development among your team by encouraging them to seek new knowledge, acquire new skills, and face new challenges head-on. Provide opportunities such as training sessions, workshops, mentorship programs, or mentorship partnerships.

6. Celebrate Successes and Learn from Failures: When rewarding achievements or milestones, celebrate to boost morale and motivation. Similarly, when failure occurs, promote an environment for learning by discussing what went wrong, identifying lessons to be learned, and making necessary improvements going forward.

7. Promote Well-Being and Work-Life Balance: Put the well-being of your team members first when it comes to work-life balance. Encourage self-care practices, provide mental and physical well-being resources, and be flexible when it comes to work arrangements.

8. Encourage Collaboration and Teamwork: Promote an atmosphere where team members support and rely on one another, promote cross-functional cooperation, increase knowledge sharing among staff members, and recognize and reward teamwork as appropriate.

9. Provide Feedback and Recognition: Give regular constructive feedback to assist your team members with personal development, then recognize and acknowledge their efforts and achievements to build morale while creating a resilient mindset.

By implementing these strategies, new leaders can foster an environment in which their team members can respond quickly to change while adapting and innovating in response to obstacles and setbacks.

Effective Problem-Solving Strategies

Challenges often necessitate leaders to implement effective problem-solving strategies. This may involve gathering relevant information, involving key stakeholders, brainstorming possible solutions, and assessing them carefully before making informed decisions about which option will work best. By employing effective problem-solving techniques effectively, leaders can overcome obstacles and drive positive change.

Effective problem-solving skills are indispensable. Here are a few strategies to enhance your ability:

1. Assess the Situation: Take time to thoroughly understand the issue by collecting relevant information and determining its root causes. Ask questions, gather perspectives, and consider potential repercussions.

2. Define the Problem: Make sure everyone is on the same page by clearly outlining your problem statement and breaking complex issues into manageable components for easier problem-solving.

3. Generate Alternative Solutions: Promote brainstorming sessions to generate multiple potential solutions and foster an environment in which team members feel safe expressing their ideas and perspectives.

4. Evaluate Options: Evaluate potential solutions according to their feasibility, effectiveness, and alignment with organizational goals. Consider both potential risks and benefits associated with each option before selecting one as your solution.

5. Make Decisions: Evaluate all options carefully to choose the one most suited to you, making sure key stakeholders have input and buy-in from diverse perspectives.

6. Implement Your Solution: Once a solution has been selected, create an action plan to implement it successfully. Assign roles and timelines to assigned employees while also setting up clear communication channels to ensure the successful execution of this task.

7. Monitor and Adapt: Regularly evaluate the progress of an implemented solution and gather feedback from relevant stakeholders, being flexible enough to modify your approach if necessary to reach desired results.

8. Learn from Experience: Take time to evaluate the results of your problem-solving efforts and identify key lessons learned. Apply these insights towards strengthening your problem-solving skills for future challenges.

Effective problem-solving skills involve combining analytical thinking, creativity, and collaboration into your strategies for efficient problem identification and resolution. Practice these regularly to maximize the efficiency with which issues can be identified and resolved efficiently.

Conflict and Difficult Conversations: Conflict and difficult conversations are an unavoidable reality in difficult circumstances, which require strong interpersonal skills from leaders in order to effectively navigate them. By directly and constructively addressing conflicts, they can find resolutions while maintaining positive working relationships.

Building strong interpersonal skills is crucial for success.

Here are some effective methods of honing and honing these abilities:

1. Active Listening: Practice active listening by fully immersing yourself in conversations, maintaining eye contact, and showing a genuine interest in what others have to say - this helps build rapport and understanding between you.

2. Empathy: Put yourself in their shoes and seek to understand their experiences, emotions, and perspectives. Show compassion by acknowledging their feelings and showing that you care about their well-being.

3. Effective Communication: Strengthen your communication skills by being clear, succinct, and assured in your messages. Adjust your style according to individual and situation needs while remaining open for feedback.

4. Cultivating Relationships: Foster positive relationships by building trust and showing integrity. Be approachable, supportive, and respectful towards team members and colleagues.

5. Emotional Intelligence: Cultivate your emotional intelligence by becoming aware and managing your own emotions while being sensitive to and understanding those of others - an approach that will create an ideal work environment.

6. Conflict Resolution: Learn how to approach conflicts constructively by listening carefully and seeking consensus before creating mutually beneficial solutions. Encourage open communication and address any potential disputes promptly.

7. Continuous Learning: Take part in personal and professional development activities like attending workshops, reading books, or seeking mentorship to further your knowledge and skillset in interpersonal interactions. This can help broaden your horizons.

Remember, mastering interpersonal skills takes practice. Be patient with yourself as you search for opportunities to apply these abilities in various settings.

Best Practices for Negotiation and Persuasion

Negotiation is an integral skill in effective leadership. No matter, if it involves colleagues, clients, or stakeholders, understanding its principles and techniques, is vital to reaching mutually beneficial results and building stronger relationships. In this chapter, we'll look at best practices for negotiation and persuasion by drawing from psychological principles such as communication theory, ethics, and communication research.

Preparing for Successful Negotiations

Successful negotiations require careful preparation. Before entering any negotiation, it is crucial to clearly outline your objectives, comprehend the needs and interests of both parties, research potential solutions/alternatives, and form a game plan to increase the chances of favorable outcomes. Once this step has been completed, focus on building rapport and trust through communication strategies that demonstrate commitment.

Building Rapport and Establishing Trust

Rapport and trust building are integral to successful negotiations, with people more likely to reach agreements when they feel connected with someone they trust and feel at ease negotiating. To establish rapport, engage in active listening, show empathy, and find common ground, trust can then be established through fulfilling commitments, being transparent in negotiation processes, and maintaining integrity during discussions. Here are five effective strategies leaders can utilize to foster them.

1. Active Listening: Show genuine interest and attentiveness by actively listening to another's concerns, ideas, and perspectives - it shows respect while creating trust by making them feel heard and understood.

2. Communication: Cultivate an environment of open and transparent communication by clearly outlining your expectations, goals, and limitations while encouraging the other party to do the same. This will establish trust while building mutual understanding.

3. Mutual Respect: For successful negotiations, treat both parties with dignity and professionalism throughout the negotiation process. Show respect for their opinions, acknowledge their expertise, and avoid personal attacks or confrontational behaviors. Doing this builds trust that leads to constructive dialogues.

4. Consistency and Reliability: Show consistency and reliability in all your actions and commitments, such as keeping promises, meeting deadlines, and following agreements made. Demonstrating this type of reliability helps build trust and establish credibility between the parties involved.

5. Empathy and Understanding: Show empathy towards the other party's needs, concerns, and challenges by placing yourself in their shoes to find mutually beneficial solutions. By showing empathy and understanding, you create rapport and foster a positive negotiation environment. Once trust has been built, effective communication and active listening become essential components in successfully navigating negotiations.

Effective Communication and Active Listening in Negotiations

Communication is at the core of successful negotiations. This involves clearly expressing your thoughts, actively listening to what others are saying, seeking clarification when needed, and seeking clarification as necessary. Nonverbal cues such as body language and tone of voice play a significant part in negotiations, as non-verbal cues influence communication during talks.

By practicing active listening and clear and concise communication, you can foster understanding and create an environment conducive to collaboration while negotiations progress toward finding win-win solutions that benefit all parties involved.

Negotiations Should Focus on Win-Win Solutions

Negotiations should aim for win-win solutions where both parties feel satisfied with the outcomes, which requires both parties to be willing to collaborate and explore creative options that meet everyone's interests and needs. By setting shared goals and seeking mutually beneficial solutions, negotiations can become a platform for building long-term relationships and fostering collaboration, but sometimes obstacles do arise; therefore, it is essential that you tackle difficult negotiations successfully in order to keep moving forward with negotiations successfully.

Obstacles and Difficult Negotiations

Difficult negotiations present their own unique set of challenges, so it is key that when approaching difficult discussions, you approach them with an open mindset to problem-solving while remaining professional and composure. Successful strategies for handling difficult negotiations include active problem-solving, reframing perspectives, and finding common ground; staying focused while being flexible and open enough to compromise may help navigate challenging situations and find solutions that meet the needs of all parties involved.

Besides negotiation techniques, persuasion plays a major role when trying to influence others during these talks.

Persuasion Techniques to Influence Others

Persuasion can be an invaluable tool for shaping other people and achieving desired outcomes. Effective persuasion techniques involve understanding the motivations and interests of the other party, providing compelling arguments supported by evidence, and using persuasive language, storytelling techniques, or ethical considerations in negotiations in order to maintain trust and integrity.

Ethics in Negotiations

Ethical considerations play an essential role in negotiations. Leaders must uphold ethical standards, practice fairness, and put all parties involved first when conducting negotiations. Honesty, transparency, and respecting boundaries are vital in building long-term relationships and cultivating trust between the parties involved. Leaders must adhere to ethical principles in negotiations while creating an atmosphere of collaboration. Preparing for negotiations is vitally important as it allows leaders to define objectives, assess alternatives, and understand the interests of all parties involved in an approach that maximizes the chances of achieving favorable results. Mastering negotiation techniques enables leaders to craft win-win solutions that satisfy all parties involved.

Enhancing Strategic Thinking and Decision-Making Abilities

Leaders need to develop a strategic mindset to help them navigate the complex business environment of today. A strategic mindset requires a long-term view, an understanding of the organization's goals and vision, and alignment with strategic objectives. Leaders who think strategically can identify future trends, anticipate challenges, and take proactive decisions to drive organizational success. Leaders can create a foundation for strategic planning and decision-making by developing a strategy mindset.

Interpreting and Analyzing Data

Making informed decisions is an important part of strategic thinking. Leaders need to analyze and interpret data in order to gain valuable insights that will inform their decisions. It involves gathering relevant data, using analytic tools to identify patterns and trends, and drawing meaningful conclusions. Leaders can use data to make evidence-based decisions and improve their chances of success. Leaders can gain valuable insights by analyzing and interpreting data. This will guide their decision-making process.

Assessing risks and identifying opportunities

Strategic thinkers are able to assess risks and identify market opportunities. They analyze the external environment and competitors to anticipate customer preferences. Leaders can create a competitive advantage and growth for their organizations by identifying opportunities. They must, however, also assess the risks and devise strategies to minimize them. Leaders can maximize their organization's potential by striking the right balance between risk and opportunity.

Leaders must assess market opportunities and risks to ensure their organization is positioned for growth. Here are some ways that leaders can evaluate these factors effectively:

1. Market Research: Perform thorough research on the market to identify emerging trends and customer needs. Analyzing customer behavior, competitor analyses, and industry reports are all part of this. Understanding the market landscape allows leaders to identify opportunities for growth and minimize potential risks.

2. SWOT Analysis: Conduct a SWOT analysis (Strengths, Weaknesses, Opportunities, and Threats) to determine the factors that impact the growth potential of the organization. This analysis will help leaders to identify the strengths and weaknesses of their organization, as well as opportunities, threats, and how to deal with them.

3. Customer Feedback: Get feedback from customers to better understand their preferences, needs, and pain points. This feedback can be collected via surveys, focus groups, or interviews. Listening to the voices and needs of customers can help leaders identify improvement areas and create strategies that meet their demands.

4. Analyze your competitors' strengths and weaknesses, market share, and strategies. This analysis allows leaders to identify ways in which they can differentiate their organizations and create a competitive edge. This analysis also allows them to anticipate the risks and challenges that competitors may pose.

These strategies allow leaders to assess the market, its opportunities, and risks. This allows them to make well-informed decisions and position their company for sustainable growth.

Set strategic goals and priorities.

In order to think strategically, you must set clear goals and prioritize them. This will guide your decision-making process and allocate resources. Leaders need to align their actions and the vision of the organization while defining measurable objectives that support the strategic direction. Setting strategic goals helps leaders give their teams a sense of purpose and direction and encourages them to work together toward a common vision. Effective leadership requires that leaders work with their teams to create strategic goals aligned with the vision of their organization. Here are five ways that leaders can work with their teams in order to achieve this.

1. Communication of the Organization's Vision: Leaders must clearly communicate the vision of the organization to their team. Share the long-term aspirations and values of the organization. Leaders can create a sense of shared purpose and direction by ensuring that everyone understands and internalizes their vision.

2. Include the team in goal setting: Leaders must involve their teams in the process of goal-setting. It can be achieved through brainstorming sessions and workshops in which team members are encouraged to share their perspectives and ideas. Leaders can harness the collective expertise and knowledge of their team to increase buy-in and help them achieve strategic goals.

3. Set SMART goals: Leaders and teams should collaborate to create SMART goals (Specific, Measurable, Achievable, Relevant Time-bound Goals) that are aligned with the vision of the organization. SMART goals help to focus and provide clarity. They ensure that goals are measurable, achievable, relevant, and time-bound. This helps the team to understand what is needed and how success will measured.

4. Leaders must encourage cross-functional cooperation within their teams. It involves breaking down silos and promoting collaboration between departments or team members who have diverse skill sets. Leaders can ensure that their strategic goals are

created with a holistic view by fostering collaboration and leveraging the expertise of the entire team.

5. Leaders must provide support and resources to the team in order for them to reach their strategic goals. It is important to allocate sufficient resources, including budgets, personnel, and technology, to ensure that the team can perform its tasks efficiently. Leaders should also provide feedback, guidance, and mentorship to team members to help them develop the skills they need to achieve the strategic goals.

These strategies allow leaders to work effectively with their teams in order to create strategic goals that are aligned with the vision of the organization. This collaborative approach encourages team members to feel ownership, motivate them, and commit themselves to the desired outcome. Prioritizing and setting strategic goals creates a road map for resource allocation and decision-making.

Implementation Strategies and Action Plans

In order to achieve goals, strategic thinking involves more than just setting goals. It also includes developing action plans and implementing strategies. Leaders need to break down their strategic goals into achievable steps, assign responsibilities, and set timelines. Leaders can provide accountability and clarity by creating clearly defined action plans. This will ensure that strategic initiatives are implemented effectively. By creating action plans and implementation strategies, leaders translate strategic goals into achievable steps that drive progress and results.

Success is based on:

- Clarity: Define clearly what you want to achieve. Avoid vague or ambiguous goals.

- Measurability: Set up measurable criteria for tracking progress and determining success.

- Achievability: Make sure that your objectives are realistic and achievable given the resources available and the constraints.

- Relevance: Make sure that every objective is aligned directly with

- Breakdown tasks: Divide the objectives into smaller and more manageable tasks.

Assigning clear responsibilities: Assign tasks to individuals or groups so that everyone is aware of their roles and responsibilities in implementing the action plan.

- Set deadlines: To maintain progress, set deadlines for each task. To create a realistic schedule, consider the dependencies between tasks.

Allocation of resources: Identify the required resources (budget, personnel, and tools) to support the plan.

- Communication: Encourage open communication and team collaboration to ensure alignment, coordination, and effective execution.

  - Monitoring and evaluation: Set up mechanisms to monitor progress regularly, track performance, and evaluate the effectiveness of the action plan.

  - Adjust as necessary to remain on track.

Leaders can create action plans that are aligned with the strategy and focused by defining clear goals and breaking them down into smaller tasks. This will increase the chances of a successful implementation of strategy and achieving desired outcomes.

Assessing and Adjusting Success Strategies

Strategic thinkers who are effective understand that it is important to evaluate and adjust strategies in order to maintain success. They monitor their progress, evaluate key performance indicators, and measure the effectiveness of strategies. Leaders can improve their strategies by evaluating them. They can also make the necessary adjustments and seize new opportunities. This iterative approach allows leaders to adjust to changing conditions and maintain their competitive edge. Leaders can remain agile and responsive by evaluating and adjusting their strategies in a dynamic environment.

Think Systemically and Consider Long-Term Implications

Strategic thinkers approach decision-making holistically and over the long term. They take into account the interconnectedness between different elements in the organization as well as the larger business ecosystem. Leaders can anticipate the long-term consequences of their decisions by thinking systemically. This perspective allows leaders to make decisions that are in line with the overall strategy of an organization and its sustainability.

Continuous learning and adapting to a dynamic business environment

Leaders must embrace a growth mindset and be committed to continual learning. They actively seek out feedback, keep up with industry trends, and stay informed. Leaders can remain ahead of the curve by continuously adapting and learning. They can also make informed decisions and guide their organization through uncertainty and change. Leaders must constantly adapt and learn to remain strategic in an ever-changing business environment.

To drive organizational success, leaders must improve their strategic thinking and decision-making abilities. Leaders can align their decisions with the strategic direction of an organization by developing a strategic mindset, analyzing data, and identifying opportunities. They can also create action plans, evaluate strategies, think systemically, and embrace continuous learning. These skills allow leaders to thrive in dynamic business environments and create a competitive advantage for their organization.

Secrets to Building High-Performing Teams

Many leaders share the goal of building a team that is high-performing. What makes these teams different? This chapter will reveal the secrets of building high-performing teams and unlocking their potential. Understanding the characteristics of successful teams is a great first step in creating one.

Teams that perform well are defined by their shared vision, goals, and sense of purpose. They have a clear understanding of what they want to achieve and are dedicated to doing so. The collective ambition of these teams fuels their motivation.

Determining roles and responsibilities for team success

It is important to clearly define roles and responsibilities in order to create a team that performs well. Each member of the team should be assigned a role that is aligned with their expertise and strengths. Leaders can optimize the performance of their teams by assigning roles that are based on each individual's capabilities. Clarity in roles is a key element in defining clear roles and responsibilities. Clarity in roles and positions is a key component of developing clear roles and responsibilities. This includes defining the scope of authority and responsibility granted to each individual in these roles. When building a team that performs well, it is important to develop comprehensive job descriptions that specify the tasks, duties, and expectations. In defining roles, it is important to have clear expectations and accountability. The team members must understand their own goals and the contribution they make to the overall objectives of the team. Clarity fosters ownership and responsibility in the team, which drives them towards success.

Creating an Environment of Trust and Psychological Safety

The foundation of a high-performing team is trust. Leaders need to create a culture that fosters trust and psychological safety so team members can express themselves, take risks, and make mistakes with no fear of judgment or negative consequences. Trust is the foundation for open communication, collaboration, and innovation in a team. Transparency, honesty, and reliability are all qualities that leaders can use to build trust. They should promote open communication, actively listen, and value the input of team members. Leaders can create an environment in which team members feel valued and supported by creating a culture that fosters trust.

Promoting Collaboration and Effective Communications

High-performing teams require collaboration and effective communication. Leaders should encourage collaboration through a culture that promotes teamwork and by breaking down silos. Members of the team should be encouraged by their leaders to exchange knowledge, work towards a common goal, and share ideas. Effective communication is essential to teamwork. Leaders need to establish clear communication channels, encourage active listening, and give timely and constructive feedback. Leaders can promote understanding, alignment, and synergy in the team by promoting effective and open communication.

Encourage Innovation and Creativity in the Team

Innovation and creativity are essential to high-performing teams. Leaders must create a culture that values diversity, encourages experimentation, and embraces new ideas. Team members must be encouraged to challenge the status quo and come up with innovative solutions. Leaders can encourage innovation and creativity through resources and support of exploration and experimentation. Also, they should reward and recognize innovative thinking in the team. Leaders can unleash the full potential of their teams by encouraging creativity and innovation.

Building Individual Strengths

It is essential to recognize and leverage individual strengths in order to build a high-performing group. Leaders must assess each member's unique talents and skills and then align their roles accordingly. Leaders can create a cohesive and well-rounded team by leveraging individual strengths. Leaders can also help team members develop and enhance their skills through mentoring, training, and other professional development initiatives. Leaders can foster a culture that encourages personal growth and continuous learning by investing in the development of individual strengths.

Building resilience and resolving conflict in teams

In any team, conflict is bound to happen. However, how the team manages it determines its performance. Leaders need to address conflict constructively and promptly, encouraging open dialogue and finding win-win solutions. Leaders can create a positive team environment by resolving conflict effectively. This will also prevent negative effects on performance.

High-performing teams must also build resilience. Leaders must help their team members learn how to adapt to changes and bounce back after setbacks. Leaders can help their teams overcome obstacles and maintain performance by fostering resilience.

Celebrating achievements and sustaining high-performance

To maintain high performance, you need to keep up the effort and give yourself recognition. Leaders must provide feedback and support to their team members so that they can stay engaged and motivated. In order to acknowledge and celebrate the hard work of your team, it is important to recognize and celebrate all achievements. Leaders can reinforce the culture of excellence by recognizing and celebrating team achievements. This will inspire them to keep performing their best.

It is difficult to build and lead a high-performing group, but this is necessary for organizational success. It takes constant effort and adaptability to build and lead a high-performing group. Leaders can unlock their team's potential and achieve success by implementing the right strategies.

Effective Time and Priority Management

Effective time management and prioritization are essential for today's leaders in a fast-paced, demanding business environment. How leaders manage their time has a direct impact on their decision-making and success. Leaders can improve their efficiency, reduce their stress, and reach their goals more easily by mastering the art of time management.

Time Management Habits and Skills Assessment

Leaders must first assess their skills and habits before they can improve time management. Self-reflection helps leaders identify areas of improvement and develop strategies to improve time management. Leaders can assess their time management abilities by analyzing the way they handle interruptions, prioritize tasks, and use technology tools. Leaders can improve their performance by identifying their strengths and weaknesses.

Setting priorities and managing your calendar

Setting clear priorities is the first step to effective time management. Leaders need to identify the most important tasks and then allocate their time accordingly. Leaders can prioritize tasks by using techniques like the Eisenhower Matrix. This allows them to concentrate on their most important activities.

The Eisenhower Matrix helps you prioritize tasks according to their urgency and importance. It is divided into four quadrants.

1. Urgent and Important: Complete urgent and important tasks first. These tasks are urgent and of high importance.

2. Important but not Urgent (Schedule). Tasks that are important but not urgent should be scheduled later. These tasks are important for long-term goals, and they require proactive planning.

3. Delegate Urgent But Not Important Tasks: If possible, delegate urgent but non-important tasks to others. These tasks require immediate attention but do not significantly contribute to your goals. They can be delegated.

4. These tasks should be minimized or eliminated if they are not urgent and important. These tasks can often be time-wasters or distractions and should be eliminated from your schedule.

It is important to manage their calendars effectively. Leaders need to schedule blocks of time that are dedicated to meetings, focused work, and their personal priorities.

Outsourcing and Delegating to Maximize Productivity

Leaders need to accept that they can't do it all. Leaders can focus more time on strategic tasks by delegating work to team members who are capable. Leaders can achieve greater productivity by empowering their teams and assigning tasks according to individual strengths. Leaders can also consider outsourcing non-core tasks to experts outside so they can focus on their core responsibilities.

Overcoming procrastination & Managing Distractions

Time management can be seriously hampered by procrastination, distractions, and other factors. To overcome these obstacles, leaders must devise strategies. Procrastination can be overcome by breaking complex tasks down into smaller, more manageable steps. Leaders should also create an environment conducive to work by turning off notifications and setting boundaries regarding interruptions. Self-discipline is also important to effectively manage time.

Effective planning and goal-setting

To optimize time management, leaders should plan and set goals effectively. Leaders can align their efforts to desired outcomes by setting clear SMART goals (Specific, Measurable, Achievable, Relevant, and Time-bound). By breaking down goals into achievable tasks and creating a deadline for completion, leaders can increase productivity. Reviewing and adjusting your plans regularly will ensure that you are making progress toward your goals.

Work-Life Balance and Integration Strategies

For leaders to be productive and maintain their well-being, they must have a good work-life balance. Leaders must prioritize their own well-being and devote time to hobbies, family, and personal activities. Work-life integration requires that you set boundaries and manage expectations with your stakeholders. Leaders can also encourage their team to put work-life balance first to create a healthy culture. Here are some ways that leaders can foster such a culture.

1. Leadership by example: Leaders must prioritize their self-care and show a balance between work and life. Leaders can encourage their employees to emulate them by setting an example of positive behavior.

2. Encourage open communication. Create an environment that is safe and supportive, where employees can feel comfortable talking about their needs and challenges in achieving a work-life balance. Encourage an open dialogue with employees and offer resources to assist them in managing their well-being.

3. Set realistic expectations. To prevent burnout, set realistic deadlines and workloads. Encourage your employees to take regular breaks, utilize vacation time and maintain a healthy pace of work.

4. Flexible work arrangements: To accommodate individual needs, offer flexible work arrangements such as remote working options or flexible work hours. Employees can better balance work and life by offering flexible working arrangements.

5. Encourage employees to participate in self-care by providing resources and organizing wellness programs. You could offer mindfulness sessions, health challenges, or fitness facilities.

6. Encourage boundaries. Respect and support personal boundaries. Discourage after-hours emails or meetings. Encourage employees to recharge and disconnect outside of work hours.

7. Recognize work-life harmony and reward employees: Appreciate and acknowledge those who place a high priority on work-life harmony. Recognize and reward their efforts and accomplishments, and create positive reinforcements for maintaining a balanced life.

8. Support and resources: Provide resources like employee assistance programs, mental support, and wellness initiatives. Make sure employees have the support and tools they need to prioritize their health.

Reflection and Continuous Improvement for Time

Time management is a process that requires continuous improvement. Leaders need to reflect regularly on their time-management practices and seek feedback from team members and colleagues. Using this reflection, leaders can identify areas of growth and make changes to improve their time management skills. Leaders can improve their effectiveness and efficiency by adopting a growth mindset and embracing new tools and techniques.

Leaders need to be able to manage their time and priorities effectively. Leaders can maximize their productivity by assessing their time-management skills, setting priorities, and delegating tasks. They can also overcome procrastination and plan effectively. Leaders can improve their leadership skills and help their teams succeed in today's dynamic environment by mastering time management.

"Unlock Your Full Potential and Lead with Impact." Embark on a transformative journey towards becoming an exceptional leader."

Leadership Mastery: Unlock your full potential and lead with impact is a message of empowerment and belief that you can become an outstanding leader. This text should serve as a constant reminder that leadership is an ongoing journey of growth and development. With the right mindset, knowledge, skills, and abilities, you can unlock and maximize your potential.

The text deliberately emphasizes the transformational nature of the journey to leadership and how to equip readers to excel as leaders. The book is designed to emphasize the importance of self-awareness, effective communication, and trust building, as well as other leadership principles that are necessary to motivate and lead high-performing teams.

The conclusion also encourages the reader to see challenges and setbacks in a positive light, as they can be opportunities for learning, growth, and resilience. The book emphasizes the importance of reflection, continuous improvement, and adaptability in a dynamic environment.

The conclusion to "Leadership Mastery - Unlock Your Full Potential and Lead With Impact" encourages the reader to believe in themselves, strive for excellence, and lead with impact and purpose. The book leaves the reader feeling inspired and motivated to begin their own leadership journey and make a positive impact in their organization and beyond.

Training Exercises

1. Scenario: "Shared Vision and Clear Goals"

Challenge: The team is given a complex problem to solve within a limited time frame. They must collectively define a clear vision and set specific goals to achieve the desired outcome. The team must demonstrate effective communication, collaboration, and alignment in working towards the shared vision.

2. Scenario: "Defining Roles and Responsibilities"

Challenge: The team is presented with a task that requires different areas of expertise. Each team member must identify their individual strengths and choose a role that aligns with their capabilities. They must work together to assign responsibilities and clearly define each member's role in contributing to the team's success.

3. Scenario: "Creating a Culture of Trust and Psychological Safety"

Challenge: The team is faced with a conflict or disagreement that threatens to disrupt their progress. They must navigate the conflict by fostering open communication, active listening, and empathy. The team members should create a safe space where everyone feels comfortable expressing their ideas and opinions without fear of judgment or negative consequences.

4. Scenario: "Fostering Collaboration and Effective Communication"

Challenge: The team is given a complex problem that requires input and expertise from multiple team members. They must collaborate effectively by sharing knowledge, exchanging ideas, and working together to find the best solution. The team must also demonstrate effective communication skills, such as active listening, asking clarifying questions, and providing constructive feedback.

5. Scenario: "Encouraging Innovation and Creativity"

Challenge: The team is presented with a situation that requires them to think outside the box and propose innovative solutions. They must encourage creativity, embrace diverse perspectives, and challenge the status quo. The team members should be empowered to take risks, experiment with new ideas, and propose creative solutions to the problem at hand.

6. Scenario: "Resolving Conflict and Building Resilience"

Challenge: The team faces a challenging situation or setback that tests their ability to bounce back and adapt. They must resolve conflicts constructively, seeking win-win solutions and maintaining a positive team dynamic. The team members should demonstrate resilience by staying focused, maintaining a positive mindset, and finding alternative solutions to overcome obstacles.

These challenging leadership scenarios will provide the leadership team with opportunities to practice and apply the key concepts discussed. They will help the team develop their problem-solving, communication, collaboration, and conflict resolution skills while reinforcing the principles of building and leading high-performing teams.

About the Author

Dennis Mullins has over 35 years of experience in the healthcare supply chain. Dennis Mullins is Vice President for Supply Chain Operations in the Southeast Region at Advocate Health. He also serves as the Chair of AHRMM. Dennis was previously SVP of Supply Chain Management at Indiana University Health. He spent eight years as the System Director for Supply Chain Integration at Baylor Scott and White. Dennis has also served in various strategic roles for HCA, including Market Operations Director at the Las Vegas Market; Director of Contracting and Supplier Diversity for North Florida Division; Director, Supply Chain for Ocala Regional Hospital and Director, Supply Chain for Providence Heart Hospital. Dennis spent ten years as a member of the Air Force, where he held various healthcare management positions. Dennis earned his Bachelor of Science at Columbia College of Missouri. He also holds an MBA and is currently working towards his Doctorate of Business Administration.

Staten House

ISBN 979-8-88940-417-0

9 798889 404170

51100

www.ingramcontent.com/pod-product-compliance
Lightning Source LLC
Chambersburg PA
CBHW070946210326
41520CB00021B/7082